PIANO
VOCAL
GUITAR

Top Hits of 2011

ISBN 978-1-4584-1501-1

HAL•LEONARD®
CORPORATION

7777 W. BLUEMOUND RD. P.O. BOX 13819 MILWAUKEE, WI 53213

Visit Hal Leonard Online at
www.halleonard.com

BORN THIS WAY

Words and Music by STEFANI GERMANOTTA,
JEPPE LAURSEN, PAUL BLAIR
and FERNANDO GARIBAY

Lyrics:

My ma-ma told me when I _____ was young, _____
Give your-self pru-dence and love your friends; _____

"We are all born su-per-stars."
sub-way kid, re-joice the truth.

* Recorded a half step lower.

4

be a drag, ___ just be a queen. ___ Don't be a drag, ___ just be a queen. ___ Don't

be a drag, ___ just be a queen. ___

born ___ this way. ___

Don't be a drag, ___ just be a queen, ___ wheth-

DON'T YOU WANNA STAY

Words and Music by JASON SELLERS,
PAUL JENKINS and ANDY GIBSON

Recorded a half step higher.

DREAM WITH ME

Words and Music by DAVID FOSTER,
JACKIE EVANCHO and LINDA THOMPSON

Slowly, with feeling

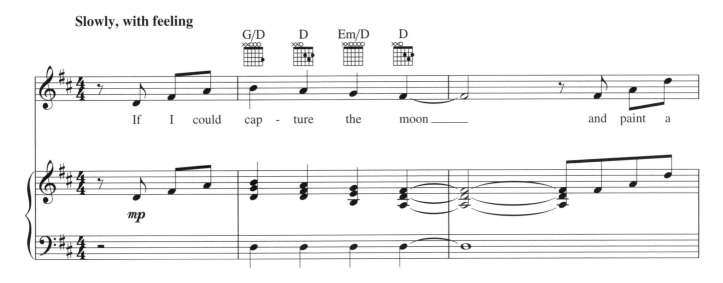

If I could cap - ture the moon ___ and paint a

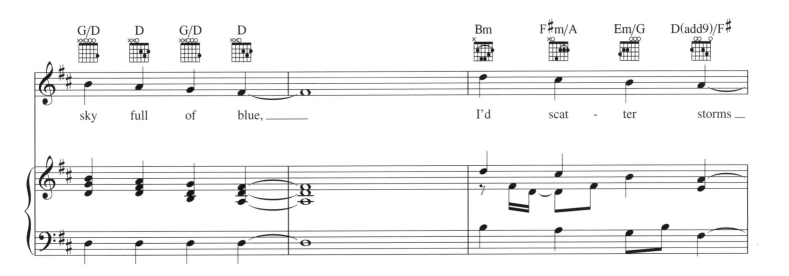

sky full of blue, ___ I'd scat - ter storms ___

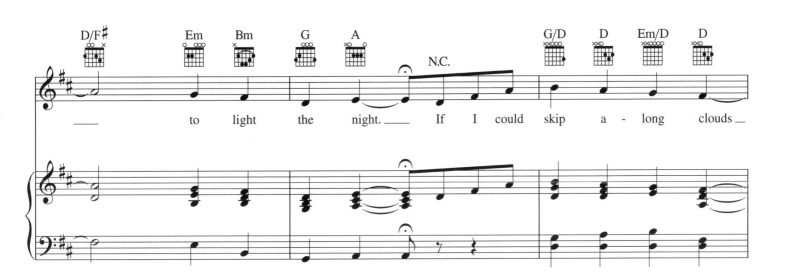

___ to light the night. ___ If I could skip a - long clouds ___

THE EDGE OF GLORY

Words and Music by STEFANI GERMANOTTA,
PAUL BLAIR and FERNANDO GARIBAY

I'm on the edge __ with you. _____

(Vocal 1st time only)

Tenor sax solo

Sax solo ends

E.T.

Words and Music by LUKASZ GOTTWALD,
MAX MARTIN, JOSHUA COLEMAN
and KATY PERRY

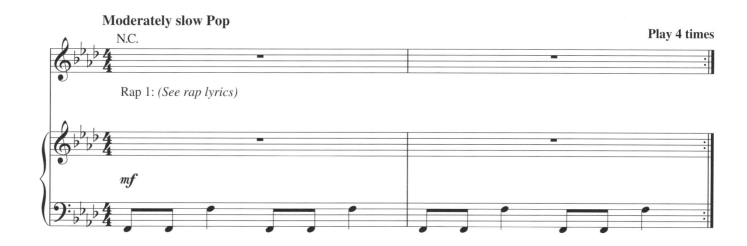

Rap 2: *(See rap lyrics)*

D.S. al Coda

CODA

ex - tra - ter - res - tri - al. ____

Rap Lyrics

Rap 1: I got a dirty mind, I got filthy ways
I'm tryin' to bathe my ape in your milky way
I'm a legend, I'm irreverent, I be reverend
I be so far u-u-u-up, we don't give a fu-u-u-...
Welcome to the danger zone, step into the fantasy
You are not invited to the other side of sanity
They callin' me an alien, a big-headed astronaut
Maybe it's because your boy Yeezy get ass a lot

Rap 2: I know a bar out in Mars
Where they drivin' spaceships instead of cars
Cop a Prada spacesuit about the stars
Getting stupid high straight up out the jars
Pockets on Shrek, rockets on deck
Tell me what's next, alien sex?
I'm-a disrobe you, then I'm-a probe you
See, I abducted you so I tell you what to do
I tell you what to do, what to do, what to do

EVERY TEARDROP IS A WATERFALL

Words and Music by GUY BERRYMAN,
JON BUCKLAND, WILL CHAMPION,
CHRIS MARTIN, PETER ALLEN,
ADRIENNE ANDERSON and BRIAN ENO

40

GOOD LIFE

Words and Music by RYAN TEDDER,
EDDIE FISHER, BRENT KUTZLE
and NOEL ZANCANELLA

Moderate Hip-Hop groove

Woke up in Lon - don yes - ter-day, found my-self in the cit - y near Pic - ca-

Recorded a half step lower.

FOR THE FIRST TIME

Words and Music by MARK SHEEHAN
and DANIEL O'DONOGHUE

Moderately slow

She's all laid up in bed with a bro-ken ___ heart, while

I'm drink-in' Jack all a-lone in my lo-cal bar. ___ And we don't know ___ how, ___

___ how we got in-to this mad sit-u-a-tion, on-ly do-ing things out of frus-tra-tion.

54

F***IN' PERFECT

Words and Music by ALECIA MOORE,
MAX MARTIN and JOHAN SCHUSTER

Moderate Pop

Made a wrong turn once or twice. Dug my way ___ out ___ blood and

fire. Bad de-ci-sions, that's al-right. Wel-come

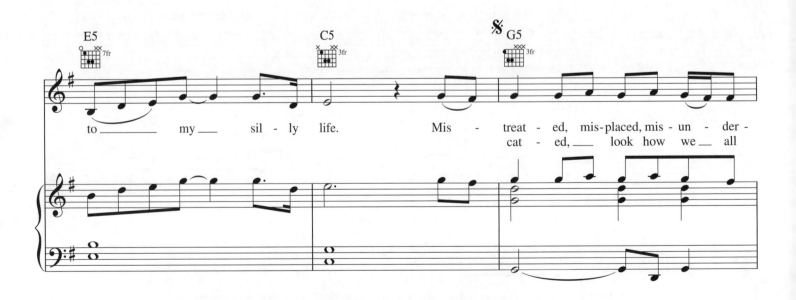

to ___ my ___ sil-ly life. Mis-treat-ed, mis-placed, mis-un-der-
cat-ed, ___ look how we ___ all

I DO

Words and Music by COLBIE CAILLAT
and TOBY GAD

Moderately fast

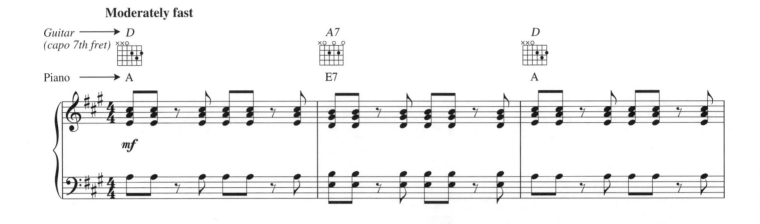

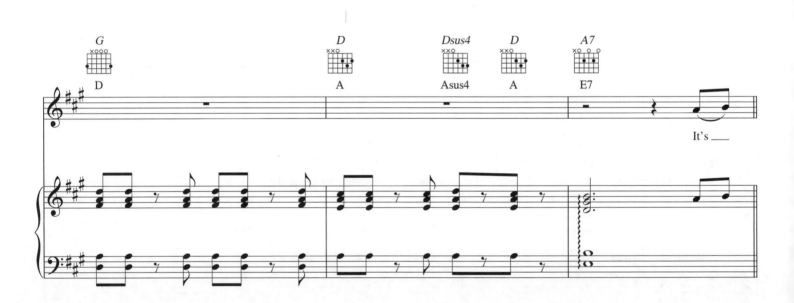

71

JAR OF HEARTS

Words and Music by BARRETT YERETSIAN,
CHRISTINA PERRI and DREW LAWRENCE

Moderate Ballad

I know I can't take one more step towards you,

'cause all that's wait-ing is re-gret.

And don't you know I'm not your ghost an-y-more,

LAST FRIDAY NIGHT
(T.G.I.F.)

Words and Music by LUKASZ GOTTWALD,
MAX MARTIN, BONNIE McKEE
and KATY PERRY

* Recorded a half step higher.

THE LAZY SONG

Words and Music by BRUNO MARS,
ARI LEVINE, PHILIP LAWRENCE
and KEINAN WARSAME

Moderately, in 2

To - day I don't feel like do - ing an - y - thing.

(whistle) _____ I just wan - na lay in my bed. _____

(whistle) _____ Don't feel like pick - ing up _____ my phone, _____ so

* Recorded a half step lower.

MEAN

NEVER GONNA LEAVE THIS BED

Words by ADAM LEVINE
Music by ADAM LEVINE

Pop Rock

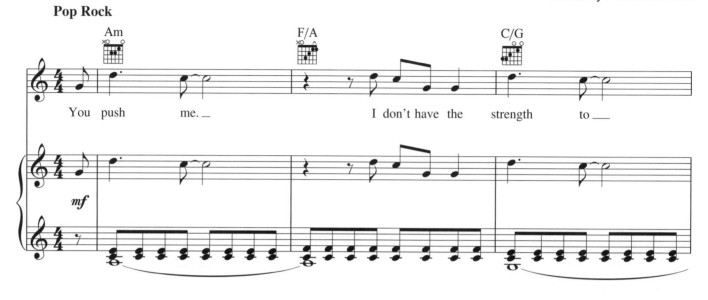

You push me. __ I don't have the strength to __

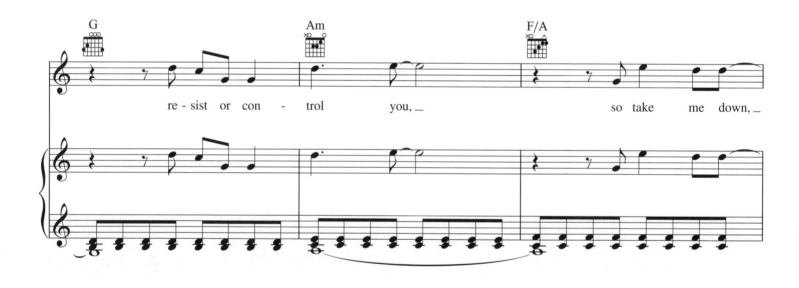

re-sist or con-trol you, __ so take me down, __

__ take me down. You hurt me, __

ROLLING IN THE DEEP

Words and Music by ADELE ADKINS
and PAUL EPWORTH

Soul groove

There's a ___ fi - re ___ start - ing in my ___ heart,

reach - ing ___ a fe - ver pitch and bring-ing me out the dark. ___

Fi - nal - ly ___ I ___ can see you crys - tal clear,

114

SAVE ME, SAN FRANCISCO

Words and Music by PAT MONAHAN,
DAVID KATZ and SAM HOLLANDER

Moderate Rock

mf

With pedal

I used to love the Ten-der-loin, ___
Ev-'ry day's so caf-fein-at- ed;

till I made ___ some ten-der coin. _____ Then I met ___ some la-dies from Ma-rin. ___
I wish they ___ were Gold-en Gat-ed. Fill-more could-n't feel more miles a-way. ___

___ We took the high-way to the "1" ___
___ So, wrap me up, ___ re-turn to send- er;

UNCHARTED

Words and Music by
SARA BAREILLES

WHAT THE HELL

Words and Music by AVRIL LAVIGNE,
MAX MARTIN and JOHAN SCHUSTER